The CANADIAN BRASS
BOOK OF FAVORITE QUINTETS

Quintet Arrangements at the Intermediate Level
with discussion and techniques

Arranged and Edited by Walter H. Barnes

We are very pleased to present a collection of some of our most requested quintets, including a wide variety of distinct musical styles, from Baroque to Dixieland. For this collection each piece has been skillfully arranged so that it retains the Canadian Brass flavor, but has been made accessible to players at many levels of experience and ability. In addition to the music, we have included a brief historical note about each selection, as well as discussion of specific technical points that will improve your ensemble playing. We sincerely hope that you will enjoy playing these wonderful pieces as much as we have over the years.

The Canadian Brass

Each part is published separately:

Trumpet I in B flat 50488966
Trumpet II in B flat 50488967
Horn in F 50488968
Trombone 50488969
Tuba 50488970
Conductor's Score 50488971
CD 50484593

The Canadian Brass has recorded the arrangements in this collection.

contents

Within an intermediate level these gradations of difficulty are indicated: E=easy, M=medium, D=difficult

a note to you

The opportunity to perform in a brass ensemble is perhaps one of the most significant in a musician's development. In a small group each individual is completely responsible for her or his own contribution to the piece of music being played. Thoughts and concepts come alive in a wonderful way when a musician realizes that four other musicians are depending on a perfect fit of the fifth part. How many times have we all heard that a great basketball or football team depends on "teamwork," but to actually experience that for ourselves through music is thrilling. To be sure we are ready for the experience, we all need to be thoroughly prepared. To help when we work with students, we always spend our time on these important points:

BREATHING: the importance of always taking full breaths
MOUTHPIECE BUZZING: every day, practice and play on the mouthpiece away
    from the instrument
TONE: your "musical fingerprint" is your tone
INTONATION: with two or more performers, intonation is critical
RHYTHM: music based on a strong rhythmic sense will always be more successful
BALANCE: a constant concern of the ensemble musician is being a team player,
    never too loud or too weak
BLEND: the beauty of brass instruments is their great blending ability

ENSEMBLE PLAYING

The real joy of ensemble performance is found when two or more performers can stylistically and sensitively play together; practicing is the quickest way to make this happen. Allow yourself to be free when you perform. Very often your fellow performers will find it much easier to play with you when you move with the music rather than "freezing" your body in place. Also, promote frequent eye contact between all the players in your group.

DOUBLING at the UNISON or OCTAVE

In our book, the French horn and trombone frequently combine at the unison, creating an entirely new sound. This must be diligently practiced by the two instrumentalists so that the style and interpretation (including tonguing, tempo, and intonation) become consistent. The trombone and tuba often double in octaves. When these octaves are perfectly in tune and balanced, a powerful effect results (which is not only very satisfying for the performers, but also for the arranger of this music).

SOLO and SUPPORTING

There are two roles in a brass quintet: solo and supporting. Although your part is always important to the whole, it is not always the solo. We want you to think of the manner in which you perform your part; dynamics, tone colour, length of notes, weight, accents, and projection all play a role in how your part will be perceived by your audience and by fellow players.

BREATHING

All too often, we hear players who try to buzz on the mouthpiece without filling their lungs with air! Sound actually starts with your first deep breath. Air is the basic fuel for the brass performer, and the proper use of this fuel ensures the quality of sound. In our books BEGINNING QUINTETS and EASY QUINTETS, we thoroughly discuss the subject of breathing, and provide exercises for mouthpiece buzzing and use of air. We consider those discussions to be required reading! In our book ADVANCED QUINTETS, we talk further about tone, suggesting that it becomes your "musical fingerprint."

PROGRAMMING

We all spend hours and hours practicing so that we can perform music we love for other people. To help you discover great music and to help you build your own concerts, music with which the Canadian Brass has had great success in public performances has been included in this book. When you put together your own program, you will find here a great range of musical styles. It is possible to experiment with playing the "classical" music of Bach and Handel, right next to early American jazz! And many other selections suitable for inclusion are found in the BEGINNING QUINTETS, EASY QUINTETS and ADVANCED QUINTETS books, all part of our CANADIAN BRASS EDUCATIONAL SERIES. Once you start feeling comfortable with this music, we encourage you to take every opportunity to perform: perform for your friends, for your families, for religious ceremonies, for your school. Just about any place you can think of to play is a good place. And most importantly, have fun with your music.

We have recorded all the selections in this book for your critical listening and study. Very often it is good practice to copy, insofar as possible, what you hear. Once you can fairly well duplicate what you are hearing, you can begin to create your own, new approach to the music. Good luck.

Your friends,

The Canadian Brass

Trumpet Voluntary

JEREMIAH CLARKE
(1673-1707)

Jeremiah Clarke was an English composer and organist at the famous St. Paul's Cathedral in London. He composed two operas, several hymns, and anthems, but the work for which he is best known today is the TRUMPET VOLUNTARY. It was erroneously ascribed to his friend Henry Purcell until 1953, when an English musicologist discovered the true composer. Originally written for organ, the grandeur of this music suited the entrance of the choir into the magnificent chancel of St. Paul's, and was exclusively used for special royal occasions.

The opening 'C' must not be underplayed, but must support and blend with the rest of the quintet. On the melodic repeat of the first 8 bars, the horn has a virtuoso part that should be brought out dramatically. At bar 20, the descending arpeggio must be strong and well-tuned. Bar 33-40, we share the melody with the Trombone; there should be a consistency of style between the two of us, both in tonguing and length of notes. Bar 52 poses some difficulty. Isolate that bar in your private practice; practice it slowly and carefully before attempting a finished speed. Then perform from there to the end grandly while supporting the two Trumpets.

The Canadian Brass

1. TRUMPET VOLUNTARY

Jeremiah Clarke
(1673-1707)
arranged by Walter Barnes

F HORN

Trumpet Tune and Ayre

HENRY PURCELL
(1659-1695)

Henry Purcell was England's greatest composer of the 17th-18th century. He received his early musical education in the choir school of the Chapel-Royal, and at the age of 20 was appointed Organist of Westminster Abbey, the site of England's royal coronations. On his burial tablet in the Abbey it is written:

"Here lyes Henry Purcell Esqr. Who left this Life, and is gone to that Blessed Place where only his Harmony can be exceeded"

Purcell worked for a secularlized Church which had very recently survived the Puritan Revolution. During the Restoration period, in which Purcell wrote most of his music, secular styles of composition were imported from France and Italy by King Charles II. As a court and church composer, Purcell was obliged to write in these new, imported styles. However, some of his earlier pieces reflect the style of his predecessor at the Abbey, Orlando Gibbons. The TRUMPET TUNE and AYRE was originally written for keyboard, and is thought to have come from a harpsichord sonata.

There are two primary performance roles in a brass quintet: solo and supporting. In this selection, you serve in both capacities. In bars 1-8 and 17-24 you are supporting the 1st trumpet. Match your intonation to the Tuba, while playing your notes in a detached style. Bars 9-16 and 25-32 give you a counter-melody which should be twinned with the 2nd Trumpet, and brought to the fore. Keep the dotted rhythm very crisp (with at least a 3:1 ratio). Intonation needs special attention when you play octaves with the 1st trumpet (bars 9-10 and 13-14).

The 'Ayre' is a contrasting section which should be played very legato, in a singing, flowing style. Return to the 'Tune' with a dynamic and rhythmic change that clearly establishes the contrast. Lastly, fill up the room with beautiful French horn tone on the final two notes.

The Canadian Brass

2. TRUMPET TUNE and AYRE

Henry Purcell
(1659-1695)
arranged by Walter Barnes

F HORN

9

Canon

JOHANN PACHELBEL
(1653-1706)

Johann Pachelbel was one of the "spiritual ancestors" of Johann Sebastian Bach. Pachelbel was especially renowned for his fugues, variations (chaconnes and passacaglias), and canons. The canon is the most strict form of imitative composition. This CANON is a series of melodic variations (specifically a passacaglia) over a repeated bass line (ground bass). Pachelbel originally wrote 186 melodies above this ground bass, each two bars in length. This particular transcription uses only 20 of those melodies.

"The CANON is perhaps the most famous classical composition ever written, as evidenced by record sales. Unfortunately, Mr. Pachelbel is no longer around to collect the incredible royalties that are pouring from these sales; on the other hand, Mrs. Pachelbel is delighted about it!" [Chuck Daellenbach, from CANADIAN BRASS LIVE]

The comments from each of us are the same: there must be absolute stylistic agreement among us regarding the many two-bar phrases. For an exercise, you can identify and number each of the twenty subjects in the score; you will then be able to observe which instrument has which melody. There are indeed twenty, but no one instrument plays them all. Select points in the music where different voices have the same melody at different times, then rehearse them at the same time. For example, the first Trumpet can play bars 29 & 30, while the second Trumpet plays bars 31 & 32, and so forth. Whether the melody is played legato, detached, bright, or flowing, it must be presented in the same style in every voice. When each instrument then plays the melody at the appropriate moment in the piece, it will be played in a matching style. Most importantly, be clear about the tempo before the performance begins. The Tuba sets the tempo at the beginning of the piece, so try to maintain this tempo throughout. To do so, keep listening to the Tuba as you progress through this marvellous canon.

The Canadian Brass

3. CANON

Johann Pachelbel
(1653-1706)
arranged by Walter Barnes

F HORN

Rondeau

JEAN JOSEPH MOURET
(1682-1738)

Mouret was a very popular composer in France during his lifetime, with more than 50 published works. Today, very little of his music is performed, with the exception of this RONDEAU. It was recently made popular because of its selection as the theme song for the BBC production *Masterpiece Theatre*. You will find, as we have, that it is an excellent addition to the brass repertoire.

The RONDEAU was originally a movement from "Fanfares pour des trompettes, timbales, violons, et hautbois" ("Fanfares for Trumpets, Kettledrums, Violins, and Oboes"). Rondo form is quite obvious: an "A" theme is presented in juxtaposition with other melodic themes. Specifically: A, A1, B, A1, C, D, A, A1.

You are again playing two roles in the RONDEAU supporting (the A theme), and solo (the B, C and D themes). You must use the same articulation at B, C and D as the two Trumpets use in the A theme; namely, bright and detached. Keep the pulse moving when you are in the solo role; spend time practicing alone with the Horn and Trombone, as the two of you often share the spotlight.

The Baroque period, from which the RONDEAU comes, often calls for strongly contrasting dynamic changes. This is partly achieved by instrumental color changes in the B, C and D themes, as well by normal, written dynamics. Exploit all the markings: make a 'forte' very strong and a 'piano' very quiet.

The Canadian Brass

4. RONDEAU

F HORN

Jean-Joseph Mouret
(1682-1738)
arranged by Walter Barnes

Largo

and

Hallelujah Chorus

GEORGE FRIDERIC HANDEL
(1685-1759)

> The grandeur and sustained power of Handel's oratorio style, the expressive simplicity of his melody, and the breadth and clarity of the harmonic structure form a wonderful artistic whole. He is unquestionably one of the 'great masters.' *(Baker's Biographical Dictionary of Musicians)*

We are sure you will enthusiastically agree with this statement after playing the two Handel compositions in this book. The LARGO (from the opera *Xerxes*,1738) displays one of the most sustained, singing melodies imaginable, this melody always supported by a simple harmonic bass. The HALLELUJAH CHORUS (from the oratorio *Messiah*, 1741) is best described by Handel himself. Upon completion of the "Chorus" he said, "I did think I did see all Heaven before me—and the great God himself!"

The LARGO opens with a beautiful French Horn and Trombone solo; try to think of the two instruments as one, creating a different instrument with its very own tone. To achieve this effect, you will both need to know how the other is going to play the solo so well that you must even think alike. Then concepts such as tuning, rhythm, and breathing become almost automatic. After you know the notes well, make a point of watching each other while you play to promote better musical communication. The low opening phrase is best suited to the range of the Trombone, so let the Trombone carry a little more of the weight. By bar 6, the Horn should start being more prominent since it climbs into a more comfortable range. From bars 15 to 46, you both support the two Trumpets as they pass the melody back and forth. When you reach the ending, you are again playing the beautiful melody. Try to make the ending gentle with a gradual, sustained rallentando.

The HALLELUJAH CHORUS offers completely different challenges. There are two distinct styles of playing involved in this piece: long sustained phrases (for example, bars 12-14, 25-27, 34-41, 43-46) and short, bright, and sharply tongued phrases (such as in bars 1-11,15-16,20-24). When playing the long, sustained phrases, it is important to give full time value to every note. Be sure to take frequent, large breaths so that the strength comes from the air and not from forcing.

The Canadian Brass

5. LARGO

from *Xerxes*

George Frideric Handel
(1685-1759)
arranged by Walter Barnes

F HORN

6. HALLELUJAH CHORUS

from *Messiah*

George Frideric Handel
(1685-1759)
arranged by Walter Barnes

F HORN

My Heart, Ever Faithful

and

Contrapunctus I from *The Art of the Fugue*

JOHANN SEBASTIAN BACH
(1685-1750)

We have selected two works of Bach that represent the wide range of this composer's brilliant talent. MY HEART EVER FAITHFUL is an aria for soprano and continuo from the Whitsunday (Pentecost) Cantata No. 68. The French Horn, Trombone, and Tuba provide the accompaniment for the two trumpets, who toss their phrases back and forth to each other. This is a delightful, light aria that sings of unrestrained joy.

The Art of the Fugue was written at the end of Bach's life. The complete work is a thorough study of all the contrapuntal techniques that can be applied to fugal writing. Bach died before completing the last (fourteenth) fugue. The first fugue is a simple fugue, a single subject followed by its answer. Since this is such a monumental work, we wanted to include the first, most straight-forward fugue for you in this collection. We have recorded the complete *Art of the Fugue* on the CBS recording label. We hope that you will listen to the entire work, especially after conquering this fugue yourself.

The French Horn has two roles to play in MY HEART EVER FAITHFUL. In bars 1-4, 13-16, and 25-28, the Horn is the soloist, presenting the main theme. For the rest of the piece, the Horn becomes part of the continuo with the Trombone and Tuba. Match their style with detached, bright and quiet accompaniment notes. So we are back to basics. There are only two ways to perform: either soloistically, or in a supporting role.

The Canadian Brass

7. MY HEART, EVER FAITHFUL
from Cantata No. 68

J.S. Bach
(1685-1750)
arranged by Walter Barnes

F HORN

CONTRAPUNCTUS I (from *The Art of the Fugue*) is perhaps the most difficult selection in the book. The range is comfortable, the phrases are not too long for proper breathing, and the melodic shape is always clear. But there is always a danger of mis-counting the rests. Consider the fugue to be an endless string of notes passed from one instrument to the next. In this way, CONTRAPUNCUS I is a typical fugue transcribed for five brass instruments, so not all the voices are sounding at the same time. Therefore, someone is always waiting to re-enter. While discussing the techniques used in playing fugues, we realized that the same points were equally important for each performer.

'Listen for the continuation of other people's lines, and try to come in smoothly and confidently.'

'Make sure you know when you pick up someone else's line, and do so without a hitch.'

'Listen to the tape that we have made for you, and try to learn all the other parts of the music.'

'This is one piece in which you have to stay very alert. Listen for the continuation of other people's lines.'

'Take frequent deep breaths, play long full phrases, and listen to the tape with this book.'

The Canadian Brass

8. CONTRAPUNCTUS I

from *The Art of the Fugue*

J.S. Bach
(1685-1750)
arranged by Walter Barnes

F HORN

Andante from the Trumpet Concerto

FRANZ JOSEPH HAYDN
(1732-1809)

Haydn wrote 31 concertos during his prolific career, with the "Trumpet Concerto" (1796) being the only one that is still regularly performed. The ANDANTE is the gentle, melodic second movement between two very exciting and technically demanding movements.

The last year of Johann Sebastian Bach's life is generally accepted as the end of the Baroque Period. In the Classical era that followed, form, structure and symmetrical shape became all-important. This can be observed clearly in our selection by Haydn. We have changed the key and simplified the melodic line of the concerto movement for you. But, in our recording of this book, Ron has performed the solo trumpet part in its original embellished form. You might also want to listen to the complete recording of the Haydn "Trumpet Concerto" so that you can understand the relationship of the 2nd movement to the other two.

It is important for the four lower instruments who are performing the 'orchestral' accompaniment to keep the rhythmic pulse smooth and steady. The accompanying eighth notes should match the eighth notes in the melody. Rehearse the accompanying instruments alone without the 1st Trumpet, striving for total coordination and cooperation.

There are also several fragments of melody or counter-melody for the Horn that should be brought to the fore: namely, bars 4, 11-12, 19-24, and 35-36. These bars must be played soloistically. Although it seems unnecessary, I have marked an optional breath in bar 20, since you must play strongly and flowingly from there to the rest in bar 23.

The Canadian Brass

9. ANDANTE
from the Trumpet Concerto

Franz Joseph Haydn
(1732-1809)
arranged by Walter Barnes

F HORN

Cor Royal

PHILIPP NICOLAI (1556-1608)
PETER CORNELIUS (1824-1874)

COR ROYAL (the Royal Horn) is an unusual composition in that it was co-written by composers living some 300 years apart. This new transcription for brass gives it yet another life. The "Chorale" by Nicolai (the Westphalian composer of the famous "Wachet auf") was written and harmonized as a four voice piece in 1599 to celebrate the Three Wise Men's historic journey to Israel to see the Christ child. The obbligato to the "Chorale" was written by Peter Cornelius 270 years later. Cornelius, a student and admirer of Richard Wagner, was well-known in his own time as a composer of beautiful melodies.

COR ROYAL is one of the most simple, but beautiful French Horn solos in the entire brass quintet repertoire. This work was originally written for the voice, and should therefore be played in a vocal manner. You will find that music originally conceived as vocal music almost always fits the brass instrument perfectly. The length of phrases to be sung have the same air requirements that you have on the horn. Experiment playing this solo while standing, making sure that your right hand is still properly positioned in the bell. Shape each phrase with dynamics and take time at the cadences; consider them almost 'grand pauses' for dramatic effect. In order to keep your quintet happy, learn this selection well before the five of you attempt to play it together.

Listen carefully to our recording of this selection; church acoustics helped to achieve a very dramatic effect. If you have a chance to perform this selection in a good acoustical building, such as a church or synagogue, project to the farthest wall and the tallest arches. Build drama. This simple melody, with its even simpler accompaniment, can be the most dramatic and best received piece for Horn. Good luck.

The Canadian Brass

10. COR ROYAL

chorale by Philipp Nicolai (1556-1608)
obbligato melody by Peter Cornelius (1824-1874)
arranged by Walter Barnes

F HORN

Sakura & Kimigayo

Traditional Japanese

The Canadian Brass has made many tours to the far East, even performing our music on the famous China Wall! It is in Japan, though, that we feel most at home. We have met many fine musicians there, and have had the opportunity to sample a great deal of Japanese traditional music. What seems unique to us about Japanese culture is the blending of so-called western music with local traditional music. It is not unusual to find modern music being played on traditional instruments, and conversely, traditional music being played on modern instruments. It is with the latter in mind that we have included two songs in this book which are very well known by all Japanese. KIMIGAYO is the "Prayer to the Emperor," and SAKURA is the famous folk song, "Cherry Blossoms." KIMIGAYO is to be used much as we would use the American or Canadian National Anthem, while SAKURA is excellent program material to be used in any performances that you give.

These two Japanese songs will give you wonderful opportunities to investigate what we consider to be our main, basic performance points for brass players.

1. AIR SUPPORT: This is the key element in all brass playing. When you get a chance, refer to our BOOK OF BEGINNING QUINTETS (the Green book) in which the first two pages talk of air support. For all brass playing, large breaths and frequent breaths are essential for good tone and tuning.
2. LISTENING: We have talked about listening throughout this book. We urge constant, careful listening to your fellow players for dynamics, blend, tuning, tempo, pulse, and doublings.
3. TIMING: Timing of notes and rests, especially the longer ones. Timing of entries and breaths, so that you are at one with your other ensemble players. Timing of thoughts and rehearsal needs, so that you are not at odds with your fellow players.
4. TONE: Your tone is your 'musical fingerprint'; only you possess that sound, only you can improve it, and only you can project that tone to your audience. Practice in front of a mirror where you can watch yourself breathing. Also, find an extremely reverberant room in which to practice from time to time (such as a concert hall, gymnasium, church, or even large bathroom) so that you can enjoy the really large sound you can make.
5. TUNING: In every text in this book, we have talked about tuning. You might have the greatest tone, but the moment you begin performing with another musician, let alone four others, intonation becomes most important. Good Intonation or tuning is only possible when you are using good air support and carefully listening to your colleagues.

We want you to be the best you can, and these five points will surely help.

The Canadian Brass

11. SAKURA
(Cherry Blossoms)

traditional Japanese
arranged by Walter Barnes

KIMIGAYO
(Prayer to the Emperor)

traditional Japanese
arranged by Walter Barnes

F HORN

Farandole from L'Arlesienne Suite No. 2

and

Toreador Song from Carmen

GEORGES BIZET
(1838-1875)

French composer Bizet is particularly remembered today for two major works: *L'Arlesienne Suite No. 2* and the opera *Carmen*. We have chosen the most famous selection from each of these masterpieces for your quintet. Both works were written near the end of Bizet's life and feature the warmth and feeling of southern Europe. They are examples of "visual" music for brass quintet, and represent the Romantic period well.

The FARANDOLE demands a feat of endurance from the French Horn player! But the more you play the piece, the greater will be your endurance. You are in a strong supporting role for the first 16 bars, changing to the melody around which everyone else pivots. The lower brass re-introduce the first melody—now in a major key—at bar 34. Notice your dynamic change; it should sound strong but independent, almost like arm wrestling between two matched opponents. At bars 63-64, you enter a dialogue with two of your friends; the style of playing must be identical. Finish with a flourish!

The TOREADOR SONG is the opposite of FARANDOLE. Throughout, you are in a supporting role. The short notes should be very staccato and percussive. Isolate and practice the run at bar 41. Pay attention to the slurs at bars 53-54; they should be similarly played by everyone. Bar 60 is great for us Horn players: good range, good notes, and good accents. Have fun.

The Canadian Brass

12. FARANDOLE
from L'Arlesienne Suite No. 2

F HORN

Georges Bizet
(1838-1875)
arranged by Walter Barnes

13. TOREADOR SONG
from *Carmen*

F HORN

Georges Bizet
(1838-1875)
arranged by Walter Barnes

Hava Nagila

TRADITIONAL ISRAELI

HAVA NAGILA was originally a wordless Chassidic melody dating from the end of the nineteenth century. Chassidics were extremely orthodox Polish Jews. This song is most closely associated with the new state of Israel, as well as the national dance of Israel, the Hora.

Everyone in the quintet gets a share of the melody in this arrangement, and everyone plays a supporting role as well. The accompaniment must be bright and short. The scoring in bars 41 through 53 is extremely effective if everyone meticulously observes their entries. There is an excellent Tuba counter-melody with the first Trumpet beginning in bar 57; this same bar is the start of a faster tempo. If one of your Trumpet players can obtain a Piccolo Trumpet, then the excitement of the dance will be even greater in bar 65. The ending is most effective if you rehearse a slight accelerando, but you must stay together as one voice. Enjoy!

The Canadian Brass

14. HAVA NAGILA

traditional Israeli
arranged by Walter Barnes

F HORN

Just a Closer Walk

arranged by DON GILLIS

This arrangement was written specifically for us to use at the beginning of our performances. Either listen to our recording <u>Canadian Brass LIVE</u>; or better still, watch our video of the same name.

In JUST A CLOSER WALK and in AMAZING GRACE, knowing a bit about the stylistic history can be helpful to ensure an appropriate performance. In times of slavery in the southern United States, death to the black person meant freedom. Death allowed a slave to 'cross the River Jordan in the Sweet Chariot, to meet God and Jesus.' During the long funeral procession out of town (since blacks were not allowed burial within the city limits) friends sang and played hymns. For variety, these hymns were played with improvised accompaniment. In this way jazz and dixieland were born. Consequently, in the presentation of both selections, you should feel a freedom of rhythm in your performance. This time the dotted eighth/sixteenth note combination needs to be played like a triplet (2:1 ratio). The melody must always be in the foreground and the accompaniment supportive. Slight bends are a nice effect in this music for all instruments, and can be applied to long notes to make them more conspicuous. After you have mastered JUST A CLOSER WALK, try playing it while you march—two steps to each bar. This will certainly aid the rhythm, and could even serve as an entrance piece for your own concerts. (A longer version of JUST A CLOSER WALK is published in our red CANADIAN BRASS ENSEMBLE SERIES series—available from your music dealer.)

The Canadian Brass

15. JUST A CLOSER WALK

traditional American
arranged by Don Gillis
adapted by Walter Barnes

F HORN

Amazing Grace – Dixie Style

a la CANADIAN BRASS

Please read the notes for the preceding selection JUST A CLOSER WALK. The "dixie" style is imperative.

The history of this song is interesting. An American, John Newton, was a slave trader for twenty years, and a regular frequenter of taverns and bars. But, as life is ever-changing, he was converted to Evangelical Christianity, moved to England, and became a Minister of the Gospel in Liverpool. He wrote the words that have made this melody famous, and which brought it from the beer halls to the gospel halls, and, back home to the black funeral processions of New Orleans!

AMAZING GRACE—DIXIE STYLE features the 2nd Trumpet, with two unaccompanied solos, one of which opens the piece. You and the rest of the Quintet enter in bar 16. The triplets, which you play through to 31 with the Trombone and the Tuba, must be very clipped, bright, but unobtrusive, so that the two Trumpets can be dominant. Again, supportive playing. At bar 66, you and the Trombone echo the two Trumpets; all four of you must play in the same style, length of note and with the same tonguing. Bars 69-72 is a duet with the Trombone; again, identical style must be presented. Bar 81 is probably the most difficult chord to tune in this entire book — Beware!

We know that you and your Quintet will enjoy this simplified version of Luther Henderson's arrangement which we have recorded on our album BASIN STREET BLUES.

The Canadian Brass

16. AMAZING GRACE

traditional American
arranged by Luther Henderson
adapted by Walter Barnes

F HORN